THE ART OF MILITARY

MINDSET IN SALES

Unclassified Edition

THE ART OF MILITARY MINDSET IN SALES

Copyright © 2017 by Jorge Rios

All rights reserved

Dedication

This book is dedicated to my wife Lena, my son Michael, my son Max, my best friend Erez, Kristin and Lilly.

Special dedication also goes to all the veterans of the armed forces past, present and future.

Table of Contents

Chapter Ten

BE INSPIRED!

Chapter One
INTRODUCTION

A man whose job involves selling or promoting commercial products, either in a store or visiting locations to get orders is usually referred to as a salesman. While a soldier is someone who serves in the army, he protects the interest and constitution of his country. These are two different occupations and one might not see any correlation between them. However, for a soldier, someone who has gone through military training, I see the two occupations differently, I see their similarities. There are certain skills or techniques known in the 'military world', that can be of great importance in the 'civilian world', especially in becoming a successful salesman.

This book outlines how you can become technically and tactically proficient in sales. The sales techniques and training are based on experiences, knowledge, and skills that I developed during my active duty with the United States military. While serving on combat operations with the Army in Iraq for two years I learned physical and mental toughness that made me a strong and effective soldier. Upon returning from combat with the Army I realized that many of the skills I learned could be applied to salesmanship in the civilian world. This book is all about transferring those skills discovered in the Army, which I like to call 'the military mindset,' to the civilian setting of sales.

You do not need to have prior military experience to utilize these sales training techniques and develop the skills that are elaborated; however, if you have served in the military, the training and techniques will be even easier to learn. Developing new skills will sharpen your ability to perform productively in the sales world, enabling you to sell any product or service to anyone anywhere. You will learn how to adopt the military mindset and apply it on the job as a salesman. Best of all, the cognitive processes involved in the sales technique will enable you to complete your top mission: the sale.

Chapter Two
SOLDIER TO SALESMAN TO SOLDIER

During basic training, soldiers are conditioned physically and mentally to endure hardship, discomfort, even pain. This conditioning is mainly for the purpose of combat operations and to gain a clear and concise capacity for decision-making under the most stressful life-threatening situations. Developing strength and perseverance in the face of adversity is an essential skill in the world of sales as well. Although the scenarios are not as harrowing, the salesperson must develop toughness, keep focused on the mission, use insight to understand and influence the customer, and maintain resilience to the customer's resistance or outright rejection.

As a soldier and as a salesman, your position or place in the world is your identity. You must without a shadow of a doubt understand who you are, what your mission is and what your goals are. The objective of military personnel is completely clear: to defend the Constitution of the United States of America against any enemies, foreign or domestic, even when this involves the possibility of sacrificing one's life. The salesman can learn from the military objective by serving the goal of the sale wholeheartedly, even when it means sacrificing one's comfort.

Unfortunately, after leaving the military, many veterans lose track of how to continue to use the amazing skills they learned as a soldier. The book is intended to rekindle the excellence found in the military in the world of sales. The average civilian has not been trained mentally to be so strong that they will never give up and will never surrender. Sadly, in the course of civilian life, civilian people often give up easily. Unlike the military, in civilian life there is no oath, no reasoning, no dedication, and no loyalty to anything besides the individual and their family. Discovering a larger purpose for living and making a serious commitment to your work vastly amplifies the effectiveness of the salesman.

When something is uncomfortable or daunting, most people tend to give up. They do not want to suffer or experience pain or be uncomfortable. But the military teaches us that persevering through discomfort leads to a greater capacity for accomplishments and a greater sense of fulfillment. As a salesman you will likely encounter great resistance and will often be discouraged or tempted to be swayed from your goal. Success will only come through maintaining commitment to the mission, being steadfast and unwavering in the face of adversity. This is the essential first step one must take to become an effective salesman. You must commit to the job, to the purpose and mission of the sale.

Chapter Three

SELF-WORTH

From day one, the first objective of military training is to instill strength and self-worth. We do not buckle or lose strength or become weak when we encounter adversity or those things that would normally crumble average people.

We do not quit when things are challenging.

We find the strength deep inside ourselves.

We look our challenges straight in the eyes and conquer them.

We see our ultimate goal and feel the satisfaction of being a winner.

When things become difficult we rise to the challenges, and we enjoy them.

As a salesman, whether you've been around for one day or twenty years, you should be proud of who you are. Our competitive culture makes us feel we need to be special and above average to feel good about ourselves, hence; comparing ourselves (or our achievement) to several other people (or their achievements). But what I need you to see here is how you can look inwards and appreciate who you are. Self-worth is instilled in every soldier, it's not achieved by comparing one soldier to the other but it is seen as a common quality every soldier should have, no matter the rank or achievement in the military. Self-worth actually helps you serve better. If for instance, working in a particular organization or at a particular capacity, can make people respect you and see you differently, you being aware of this will affect your carriage around such people.

Now think about this: what if there is no United States Army…no soldiers? I am sure you can imagine the consequences. Now think about this too: what if there are no salesmen…? Will products and customers not suffer? You are a great asset both to the customers and to the services you're providing or the product you're selling; forget those time you were turned down, you are filling a void.

I came across this Leo Bogee, Jr.'s explanation of what self-worth really is;

Before defining self-worth, let's take a look at the definition of self-esteem. The World Book Dictionary, a Thorndike-Barnhart Dictionary, defines self-esteem as "thinking well of oneself; self-respect." The concept of someone having self- esteem was first conceived in the year 1657. It wasn't until 308 years later, 1965, that self-worth was recognized as a separate concept. Even today, many dictionaries still define self-worth as self-esteem.

If self-esteem is "thinking well of oneself," then what is esteem? Esteem is a very favorable opinion or high regard for someone or something. If someone has a very favorable opinion or high regard for someone else, then what is that esteem actually based on? The esteem is based on something someone has actually done. The person in question is being esteemed for their skills in acting, sports, politics, education, etc., or on anything that involved their ability to do something.

I view self-esteem as a measure of how well our physical or Human Self is able to perform or accomplish something. The esteem comes from sources OUTSIDE us. Although the term self-esteem implies we are esteeming ourselves, in actuality, the esteem is coming to us from another source. The criterion for esteem is determined by others. Our performance is measured against that criterion and the acknowledgment follows. The better our performance, the higher the esteem awarded to it. However, no matter how much esteem we receive based on our ability or our performance, we are not always able to accept it or to receive it.

You must be in the present to receive self-esteem.

For example:

Someone has just received the highest award in their field of endeavor. They are publicly acknowledged in newspapers, magazines, and on television. They are invited as a guest on all the major TV Talk Shows; in other words, they are placed on top of the world. Then without any warning, this person who is the envy, role model, hero, or champion of millions of esteeming people, commits suicide.

How could they possibly do such a terrible thing? Their "self-esteem" was as high as it could possibly be and yet it didn't save them.

This example is no longer the exception to the rule; it is the rule. How can that be true with all of the focus on self-esteem courses and programs? How can that be true with the flood of people being licensed in the psychiatric and psychological fields of medicine each year? The answer can be simply stated, but not simply understood. As matter of fact, the answer was stated in the opening paragraph. Self-worth is not self-esteem!

So, what is self-worth?

The World Book Dictionary defines self-worth as "a favorable estimate or opinion of oneself; self-esteem." The World Book Dictionary recognizes the distinction in concept; however, it does not recognize the distinction in meaning. I view self-worth as a measure of the availability of our Spirit or Being to believe in ourselves. Self-worth comes from a source on our INSIDE. We create it through Faith, by acting on the singular belief that we matter. Self-worth is the foundation of our ability to believe in ourselves.

Self-worth comes from appreciating yourself as a salesman; don't ever look down on that. In the second chapter, I said "As a soldier and as a salesman, your position or place in the world is your identity. You must without a shadow of a doubt understand who you are and what your mission is." The understanding of who you are and what you do is where you draw strength, self-worth and self-respect.

Now that you know your place in the world and have an understanding of the 'Never Give Up' military mindset, it's time to start to build your tactical sales skills.

Chapter Four
THE SUCCESSFUL SALESMAN

It cannot be overly-emphasized that to become successful in sales you must thoroughly understand that your mission is to complete your objective and sell the product, service or good. To be a successful salesman you must vow to never give up, to never surrender, and to overcome whatever obstacles that are placed before you. In short, you must be entirely committed to completing your mission and selling to your client.

Does this mean that you will land the sale every single time? -Of course not. Does this mean that people will sometimes refuse your sales attempts? Absolutely, but this does not mean that you will deteriorate. It does not mean that you will give up on your sales demonstrations and pitches. You must be committed to becoming stronger, because you understand your self-worth (discussed fully in chapter four). You look in the mirror and feel pride in being a salesman. Just as a soldier looks in the mirror and is proud to serve his country, you can be proud to serve your company. Just as a soldier wears a uniform to represent his country, you wear your suit and your professional attire to represent your product, service or good.

To be a successful salesman you must know who you are and appreciate yourself. You must feel good about what you're doing and believe in your product. You must believe in your mission and your sales no matter what anyone tells you. You must be completely committed to your mission because you have the self-worth of a soldier who is a salesman.

There are certain traits enumerated by the Canadian Professional Sales Association (CSPA); which every salesperson must possess. These are also traits you find in a soldier.

Empathy: Empathy is the ability to identify with customers, to feel what they are feeling and make customers feel respected. Empathy is NOT sympathy, which involves a feeling of loyalty with another individual. It is more than understanding their concerns from an objective standpoint. A salesperson showing empathy can gain trust and establish rapport with customers by being on their side and not appearing judgmental. Empathy allows the salesperson to read the customers, show concern, and clearly demonstrate his or her interest in providing a proper solution.

Focus: A person with focus is internally driven to accomplish goals and can stay attentive to one topic. Focused individuals are more demanding of themselves than other people and they are self-motivated. They are able to organize themselves and recognize what needs to be done in order to achieve their goals.

In a salesperson, focus produces best results when it is balanced with empathy. You then see a person who listens and identifies with the customer while keeping focused on set goals, and who is able to translate these goals into solution for the customer.

Responsibility: A person with a strong sense of responsibility does not place blame on other people when placed in a difficult situation. This type of person, referred to as an "agent", gets things done and when obstacles arise, accepts any errors or omissions that have occurred. He or she does not get defensive nor do they try to blame the situation on circumstances or on other people by making statements such as, "it's not my fault boss that consumer confidence has declined in Afghanistan (or Iraq)."

Optimism: A salesperson with healthy amount of optimism can be described as someone who is slow to learn helplessness. This person has persistence-a trait that is critical in the sales world because of the frequency of rejections salespersons experience. In the face of failure, some people throw their hands up in the air and resign themselves to the disappointment because they feel helpless to change the situation. Others, however, see themselves as being more resilient and that a customer's refusal is NOT a rejection of themselves personally, but of the opportunity being offered. Salespersons who possess a large amount of optimism like themselves and when they encounter failure, although disappointed, it does not destroy their positive view of themselves. They consider themselves still in the running and able to turn the situation around. They believe that they can make things better by using a different approach, or by trying again.

Ego-drive: Ego-drive is similar to optimism in that both traits require persistence for the purpose of succeeding and above all winning. It's all about competitiveness. When a person hangs in there with fists clenched and a teeth gritting appetite to succeed at his or her goal, you see a powerful ego-drive. This person is self-motivated and a self-starter with clear ideas of what he or she wants to achieve.

Chapter Five
LOYALTY

Having loyalty to your product and service will skyrocket you in sales to a level that you've never imagined.

When we have loyalty to our family our units our company or any organization, this loyalty runs so deep that no one may say or do something that may disturb the integrity in the structure of our niches. And when we have loyalty to our product or service, we have the belief so strong in it that we come to know who we are, we will understand our mission and we will maintain such loyalty to our product, service and our customers too.

This loyalty will help you surpass any kind of obstacle that may be in your way for instance if you have to stay longer on a project; you have loyalty and respect for your organization, for your sales, for the product you are selling or service you are rendering, for whatever project you have embarked on, such that loyalty becomes second nature to you in business.

Soldiers have loyalty to their units, their battalions, their squads and their team so much that if they have to give their lives for the better and for the protection of their units or their fellow soldiers, they will. Of course we're not in the extreme that we will give our lives for our sales or product or service but this commitment, this drive, this loyalty, this level of perseverance, is one that we need to reach in order to be able to be at the highest level of achievement.

Loyalty runs so strong in the fibers of our being that it is a part of who we are. The loyalty that we have for each other, the loyalty that we have for the sales, the loyalty we have for our product.

So how can I have loyalty for my product, service or good?

First and foremost you must have the loyalty that you know everything about your organization and product in depth that you know it's like you know the back of your hand or even better than you know the back of your hand.

Loyalty is a virtue that every individual should possess, it's very important in any business. Loyalty to your customers helps in building satisfaction and trust toward your service and products. When you are loyal to your customers, they will be loyal to your business; your products or services. There will be an assurance that these customers will patronize your products, thus increasing your sale and opening several relationships, as you close several deals.

Loyalty is one virtue that people find difficult to achieve. It requires a resolution not to deviate from dealing with people on this term. In a relationship, loyalty is also needed because it creates commitment and dedication to someone you care for. Loyalty stems from caring for, believing in someone, something or a cause. Believing in what you do and who you are, believing in your organization and your product or service. If you love somebody for instance, you will make sacrifices to strengthen the relationship and make it work. That sacrifice will usually involve giving your utmost loyalty to such a person you care for. It works the same way with your responsibility as a salesman, to the organization you are working for, to the product you are selling or the service you are rendering and to your customers.

Chapter Six
INDUSTRY, GOALS & MISSION

The Industry

Americans who work in sales-related jobs other than retail sales are about 5.5 million. Those who sell the products of wholesalers and manufacturers are about 1.8 million. About 1.5 million sell services such as advertising, insurance, and securities. Almost all other industries depend on the sales industry to reach their consumers; ranging from farm produces and tons of food items to service-providing businesses, such as advertising, insurance, medicine.

Enterprise Software/Consulting Sales

This industry has a higher learning curve and is harder for beginners to break into. It is extremely lucrative if you come in with experience. Enterprise software has a significantly longer sales cycle as products/services have a much higher price tag.

Medical Device/Pharmaceutical Sales

The medical device and pharmaceutical industries both share a high learning curve. These industries are extremely competitive and very quick to fire under-performers. Usually reps are given a set list of accounts with a regional coverage. These jobs involve more travel compared to other industries. Pharmaceutical and Medical device sales reps are commonly asked to be a part of actual surgeries and drug applications to help guide physicians when using their products.

Financial Services Sales

This is a broad industry. Jobs can range from selling consumer investment plans at ING, to working at Goldman Sachs creating wealth management plans for billion dollar companies.

Real Estate/Commercial Real Estate Sales

People might want to opt for commercial real estate sector because it pays higher than residential real estate sector.

Copier/Office Technology Sales

The copier sales industry is a great starting point for any beginner salesperson. Almost 100% of businesses need some form of the product. It allows reps to build relationships with local business owners and get a ton of experience managing basic sales cycles.

Telecommunications/Security sales (B2B)

This is a very common industry for sales beginners.

Manufacturing/Consumer Goods Sales

This sector also features a shorter learning curve and as a result, a smaller pay grade. And finally,

Door to Door Sales (telecom, security, etc.).

As a soldier salesman you must pick an industry in sales. Now that you have a better understanding of the different industries offering sales jobs, you should decide which is going to be the best fit for your skill set. Your chosen industry is where you will create your masterpiece. It's where you will focus your first main mission, and manifest your own personal Army of effort and engagement. After you have mastered sales in your main industry, you will have completed the first phase of your mission. But your mission is not over yet, your ultimate mission extends to the end of your life.

It is not your job, but rather your duty to complete your mission. You are not only the soldier in your sales mission, but also the commander. How do you know what your mission is? For most of us, our goals are also missions. We all have goals, and our ultimate, highest goals are part of our mission. From here on, think of your goals as aspects of your larger life mission.

Chapter Seven

THE MISSION

Always place the mission first. The mission is sales success. It should be taken as a duty and an obligation, not an option. Most people in sales look at their jobs as an option, and there are always other options in their minds. They think it's smart to have plan A, plan B, and plan C. They think if plan A won't work, plan B will—and if plan B falls through, there's always plan C.

The way of multiple options, without a sense of commitment, is not the way of the salesman soldier—because it is not a path to becoming tactically proficient and achieving ultimate success.

The salesman soldier has plan A and sticks to it, even when things get rough. If plan A isn't working, you don't move on to plan B, you look at what is going wrong and figure out how to make it work.

Levels of Mission

In order to structure the mind like a soldier in sales, we must clearly identify our mission. When I was deployed to Iraq we had levels of missions. Within each of these levels of missions were more detailed missions.

Level 1: Invade the Iraqi government.

Level 2: Capture Saddam Hussein.

Level 3: Re-establish the Iraqi government.

In Chapter One, we covered our identity as a person, our purpose, and our self-awareness as a salesman. In this chapter we've outlined our mission, and the mission comes first—our mission to sell and achieve our daily goals, having discussed the industry.

The average person usually stops what they are doing and seeks an alternate option when obstacles arise. As soldier salesmen, we need to be strong and look forward to obstacles. We need to welcome roadblocks on the path to our achievements. Our zeal for facing and overcoming challenges makes us stronger and sets us apart from the average Joe. It is how we become so successful, how we master sales and become absolutely proficient.

The mission is not always easy or clear. Not all of your potential customers or clients will be eager to sign up and buy your product or service. You should expect to encounter challenges and difficulties at every step of your mission. More importantly, you should be prepared to deal with hardship and to persevere.

Most average salesmen will complain and moan about how hard it is to sell. They will lament at how much effort they have put forth for so little reward. To overcome this self-defeating pessimism, you need to keep the end goal of your mission in mind. Remember that your mission is not complete until you reach the end goal, until you cross all hurdles.

With awareness of an overall life mission that is composed of multiple layers of smaller missions, you understand that once one mission is completed the next is right around the corner. You understand the extent of the journey and always keep the end goal in mind.

Chapter Eight
THE GOALS

Most average people perceive their jobs in a limited manner, as a means to arrive at an end. As a soldier salesman, we understand our jobs as our duty and obligation to achieve our life mission. Relative success is experienced on a case-by-case and daily basis. But ultimate success takes a lifetime. This means that no matter what the objective or the end outcome of a day's work is, whether negative or positive, it is only a step towards our overall life mission.

What would be in your package? Where would your prize take you? How would this prize change your life? Your answers to these questions can help you discover your most important life goals. Life Coach Spotter said important things about life goals and setting such goals.

What Are Life Goals? Life goals reflect our purposes in life, as well as our various objectives. They are the driving force behind everything that we do, and they are the most important things that we want to accomplish. Your goals in life are often found in list form, detailing everything that someone wants to do before they die or reach a certain age.

These are commonly referred to as "bucket lists," which have become extremely popular over the last several decades.

Life goals include the things that we want people to remember us for after we're gone. They comprise the legacy that we want to leave behind for the generations that follow. They are the things that come to mind when we dare to dream. Put simply, life goals are the things we want to do, be, and have that are most important to us.

Do I Need Life Goals?

Life goals are much more than just targets that we shoot for throughout our lives. They are vital to the quality and direction of our lives, determining where we're going next and where we will end up further down the line.

Goals help keep us focused while providing clarity into what it is that we want most. They make us more determined to get to where we want to be and experience the things that we most desire. They open up our sense of resourcefulness, which gives us the drive to find new ideas, support systems, and tools such as technology, consultants, coaches, and innovative thinking. When you're feeling stuck or lost in life, having life goals aligns you with your own personal true north.

Goals help us channel our energy into getting what we want, and they prevent us from wasting our time on anything that takes us in the opposite direction of what we are seeking. Personal goals can also keep us accountable, which makes us responsible for ourselves and our future. This puts the power and control back into our hands and allows us to guide our lives in any direction that we choose. No dream is too big when goals are strategically set.

Most importantly, our goals in life help us to be the best possible version of ourselves, and they ensure that we live the life of our ever-expanding dreams.

Let's see the different types of goals.

Long-term goals are achieved over time as a person completes the stages of their life. People set long-term goals for themselves by envisioning what they want to be doing and where they want to be five to twenty years from the present. Then they use short-term goals to get there.

Short-term goals are ones that a person will achieve in the near future, typically in less than one year. Short-term goals are often, but not always, steppingstones on the way to achieving long-term goals. These types of goals are considered enabling goals because accomplishment of these goals will "enable" you to achieve an even greater goal.

Enabling goals usually consist of such topics as education, short-term jobs or projects, as well as valuable work experience. Each of these often contributes directly to the long-term goals a person sets for himself or herself.

But we are interested in an aspect of both short and long-term goals. Provisional goals are subdivided under short-term goals, they result in relative success. While lifetime goals are subdivided under long-term goals. They usually result in ultimate success.

Provisional Goals (relative success)

Provisional (stepping-stone) goals are usually stepping-stones to the larger goals. Typically, these are completed in less than a month. These are the types of goals you focus on a daily basis and are often used for technical improvements.

Many times these may be enabling goals that may need to be accomplished prior to the foundational goals being met. "Get a 90 or better on the Algebra test next week", which will help meet the goal of getting straight A's next semester in order to get into a good college, so that you can eventually go to medical school. However, like Foundational goals, provisional goals can be stand-alone goals with no link to a Lifetime, Capstone, or a short- term goal. This could be "paint the house", "clean the basement", or "finish a school project."

Lifetime Goals (ultimate success)

Lifetime goals are those major goals that you would like to accomplish over your lifetime. Depending on your age, these goals may be accomplished significantly later on in your life.

Typically, these goals will have accomplishment dates of ten or more years in the future. Lifetime goals may fall into one of several categories including career, education, family, financial, or just pleasure. You can have a Lifetime goal to become an accountant as well as goals of getting a Master's Degree, having four children, making ten million dollars, and/or traveling around the world.

Lifetime goals are often general at first but as you work towards them, they become more specific. The original goal of "get a job as a teacher" becomes "Get a job teaching math to high school students," which later evolves into "enter a career in teaching Trigonometry and Calculus to high school seniors." As time goes on, the more defined your goals will become. It works the same way in the sales industry.

With the awareness of your life mission, you will always strive for more and can never fail. Your true success is determined and achieved over a lifetime of effort that will involve many little failures and successes. It is only when you are 100% fully committed to your end goal, to your larger life mission, that you will ultimately win through achieving life-long success. We can never fail when we have no other option but strength, dedication and commitment to the mission.

Chapter Nine
IDENTIFYING WITH YOUR PRODUCT

The study and understanding of all aspects of your product or service must be known and studied over and over until it's a part of you like your breath.

Every video you can search online and watch, every book you can get your hands on or read online, every self-development skills you can learn. You must absorb all the information so that it becomes a part of your self-identity and your mission. Your mission must be powered by your knowledge and your self-worth; these aspects shape the way you perceive the very fabric of reality. These are the parts that are shaped in soldiers and government operatives while on their combat operations and it's why they are so strong. You can be just as strong by utilizing these skills for sales. This outline and structure will strengthen you at your core. Strong operatives have clear understanding of these outlines when it comes to their missions. Combining each part of this outline will build you into the most powerful sales man in any organization you walk into. People will appreciate your ability to sell to anyone, any time and how to always be the best.

How else can you identify with your product?

Use technology to your advantage! Use the internet! Do you know how much technology has been aiding the United States military?

Strength, valor, self-worth, loyalty are some of the qualities instilled in a soldier, but how much can he do in combat, without his assault rifle/carbine, his pistol, how about the grenade-based weapons, the DMRs and sniper, machine guns, shotguns, submachine guns, portable anti-materiel, and there are still more equipments used by the United States Army- I have not mentioned artilleries, vehicles, aircrafts, vessels and the attire.

It's common knowledge how much you can interact with your customers via social media platforms. You can interact better with your customers; rather than just have their inquiries or 'advertise' your product or service; you can do more by relating with them and registering their interest or specifications, and this is where your quality as a soldier salesman comes in- empathy. Empathy is the ability to identify with customers, to feel what they are feeling and make customers feel respected. A soldier uses his weapon but it's not about using it alone, how effectively is he using it...? As a soldier salesman, you can use technology effectively to make your work easier. There several ways you can reach your customers for instance, even when you are distance apart and he/she can still have an idea of the product you want to sell or the service you want to render.

How else can you engage the internet? I already mentioned streaming online videos to improve your skills, reading e-books or any article that add to your knowledge as a salesman. It's not enough to have weapons; soldiers are taught several tactics useful in combat, they are taught how to be skillful in handling them and how to be yet skillful and tactical in situations when they happen to be without them, they are conditioned physically and mentally to endure hardship, discomfort, even pain. This conditioning is mainly for the purpose of combat operations and to gain a clear and concise capacity for decision-making under the most stressful life-threatening situations. When I was on active duty in the Army, serving in Iraq for two years, I learned physical and mental toughness that made me a strong and effective soldier. Salesmen always end up in this situation if not all the time, in the cause of their job. Technology can only aid, but your skill-set comes from self-development, the qualities (loyalty, self-worth, strength, doggedness and determination, and so on) of a soldier salesman are virtues you work on gradually, to be a better person and to be better at what you do.

Chapter Ten
BE INSPIRED!

"Begin by always expecting good things to happen."

-Tom Hopkins

"For every sale you miss because you're too enthusiastic, you will miss a hundred because you're not enthusiastic enough."

-Zig Ziglar

"The majority of men meet with failure because of their lack of persistence in creating new plans to take the place of those which fail."

-Napoleon Hill

"Ninety percent of selling is conviction and ten percent is persuasion."

-Shiv Khera

"Self-pity is an acid which eats holes in happiness."

-Earl Nightingale

"Obstacles are necessary for success because in selling, as in all careers of importance, victory comes only after many struggles and countless defeats."

-Og Mandino

"Obstacles can't stop you. Problems can't stop you. Most of all, other people can't stop you. Only you can stop you."

-Jeffrey Gitomer

"The difference between try and triumph is just a little umph!"

-Marvin Philips

"The most unprofitable item ever manufactured is an excuse."

-John Mason

"He that is good for making excuses is seldom good for anything else."

-Benjamin Franklin

"There are no shortcuts to any place worth going."

-Beverly Hills

"Tough times never last, but tough people do."

-Robert Schuller

"Don't which it was easier, wish you were better."

-Jim Rohn

www.ingramcontent.com/pod-product-compliance
Lightning Source LLC
Chambersburg PA
CBHW070724180526
45167CB00004B/1607